D1743996

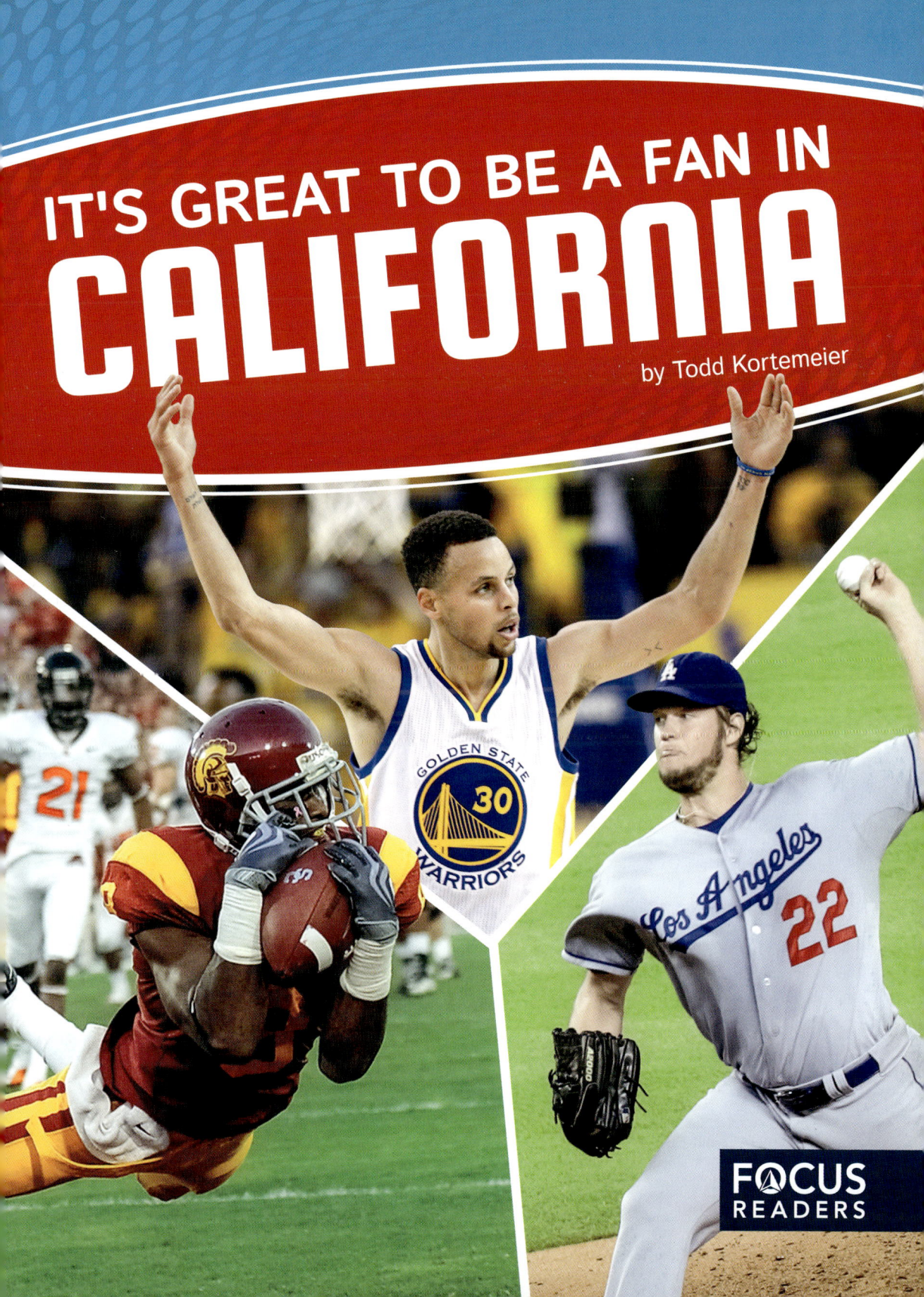

IT'S GREAT TO BE A FAN IN
CALIFORNIA

by Todd Kortemeier

GOLDEN STATE
WARRIORS
30

Los Angeles
22

21

FOCUS
READERS

FOCUS READERS

www.focusreaders.com

Focus Readers is distributed by North Star Editions:
sales@northstareditions.com | 888-417-0195

Produced for Focus Readers by Red Line Editorial.

Photographs ©: Marcio Jose Sanchez/AP Images, cover (top), 1 (top); Mark J. Terrill/AP Images, cover (left), 1 (left), 37; Lynne Sladky/AP Images, cover (right), 1 (right); oneinchpunch/Shutterstock Images, 4–5; Henry Bryan Hall/D. Appleton & Co./Library of Congress, 7; kenkistler/Shutterstock Images, 9; Red Line Editorial, 11, 19; Peieq/Shutterstock Images, 12–13; Harold P. Matosian/AP Images, 15; Ezra Shaw/AP Images, 17; Stacy Bengs/AP Images, 21; Lenny Ignelzi/AP Images, 23; Photo Works/Shutterstock Images, 24–25; Jeffrey Brown/Icon Sportswire/AP Images, 29; Ryan Kang/AP Images, 31; Peter Leabo/AP Images, 32–33; trekandshoot/Shutterstock Images, 35; Gerry Boughan/Shutterstock Images, 38–39; Galina Barskaya/Shutterstock Images, 41; dibrova/Shutterstock Images, 43; Gregory Bull/AP Images, 44

ISBN
978-1-63517-926-2 (hardcover)
978-1-64185-028-5 (paperback)
978-1-64185-230-2 (ebook pdf)
978-1-64185-129-9 (hosted ebook)

Library of Congress Control Number: 2018931661

Printed in the United States of America
Mankato, MN
May, 2018

ABOUT THE AUTHOR

Todd Kortemeier is a sports journalist, children's book author, and lifelong San Diego Padres fan. Despite living most of his life in Minnesota, he grew up listening to Ted Leitner and Jerry Coleman while dreaming of hitting like Tony Gwynn. Todd and his wife live near Minneapolis with their dog.

TABLE OF CONTENTS

CHAPTER 1

THE GOLDEN STATE

People have long come to California seeking opportunity. For sports fans, the state has no shortage of opportunities to both watch and participate in sports. California boasts more professional sports teams than any other state. The state also has some of the most successful college sports programs and hosts many major sporting events. Like the state itself, though, most of its teams are relatively young.

People come from all over the world to visit or live in California.

American Indians were the first people to settle in California. They arrived thousands of years ago. In the 1500s, Spanish explorers landed in California. It wasn't until well into the 1800s that they **colonized** the area. That's why many places in California have Spanish names.

The area changed greatly in the late 1840s. In 1847, **prospectors** discovered gold in California. By the next year, the Gold Rush had begun. Approximately 100,000 people flocked to the area hoping to get rich. At the time, California was part of Mexico. But when the Mexican–American War (1846–1848) ended, Mexico was forced to give the territory to the United States. Two years later, in 1850, California was admitted as the 31st state.

The Gold Rush spurred a population boom. By 1860, California's population had tripled to 308,000. Gold remained important, but other

natural resources took off as well. The state's agriculture industry boomed as farmers grew wheat, oranges, and other crops.

Even with the Gold Rush, California remained somewhat isolated. It was the only state on the West Coast until Oregon joined the United States in 1859. However, most of the other western territories were still decades away from statehood.

The railroad helped change all that. In 1869, workers completed the Central Pacific line. California was finally linked to the rest of the country. However, this line was most vital to Northern California, where the state's growth began with the Gold Rush. Southern California was still a quiet area of mostly small towns. Finally, the Santa Fe Railway connected Los Angeles with the eastern United States in 1885. By 1900, the population of Los Angeles had swelled to 100,000.

Growth continued statewide for most of the 1900s. Part of this was due to immigration from

➤ **THINK ABOUT IT**

Which is your favorite sports team in California? How did you become a fan?

Railroads connected California with the rest of the country.

Asia and Latin America, starting in the beginning of the century. Many immigrants worked in California's agricultural industry, and others worked in manufacturing.

Around this time, a new industry was forming in Southern California. Filmmakers saw California's sunshine, unique landscapes, and plentiful space as perfect for filming movies. In 1900, Hollywood was a small, unknown town outside Los Angeles. Today, it is the film capital of the world.

By 1950, California's population was 10 million. Between 1950 and 2000, it tripled in size. This was the highest growth rate in all of the United States. California is now the most populous state in the nation, with nearly 40 million people. Los Angeles is the state's largest city. Known as the City of Angels, it is home to four million people. Millions more live in neighboring cities.

Over the years, California's traditional industries continued to grow. New industries emerged, too. Silicon Valley, in the San Francisco Bay Area, became a technology hub in the 1980s. Today, the tech sector is strong throughout the state. California is also a popular vacation spot for people around the world. In fact, the state is the leading tourist destination in the United States.

Sports teams have also succeeded in California. As a huge state with several major cities, it has 20 professional teams that play in major leagues. California's teams are a big part of its economy and culture. Some are so popular that they have fans around the world.

CALIFORNIA SPORTS MAP

Sacramento Kings

San Francisco Giants
San Francisco 49ers

Oakland Athletics
Golden State Warriors
Oakland Raiders*

San Jose Earthquakes
San Jose Sharks

Los Angeles Dodgers
Los Angeles FC
Los Angeles Galaxy
Los Angeles Clippers
Los Angeles Lakers
Los Angeles Chargers
Los Angeles Rams
Los Angeles Kings
Los Angeles Sparks

Anaheim Angels
Anaheim Ducks

San Diego Padres

LEAGUE
- MLB
- MLS
- NBA
- NFL
- NHL
- WNBA

*The Raiders are scheduled to move to Las Vegas, Nevada, in 2020.

CHAPTER 2

MORE PEOPLE, MORE TEAMS

With its warm weather, California is a natural home for outdoor sports. The weather is also consistent, which makes it easy to schedule games. So it was no wonder that sports took off in the state.

Minor league baseball was the first organized professional sport in California. The first team was founded in San Francisco in 1878. Other teams soon formed in other parts of the state.

Baseball is one of many sports that benefit from California's weather.

But most other pro baseball teams in the United States were in the eastern and central parts of the country. Traveling to faraway states would have taken too long. As such, the California teams started their own league.

In 1902, the California League added teams from Oregon and Washington. The league then became known as the Pacific Coast League (PCL). It still exists today. Mild weather meant teams could play many games. In 1905, the San Francisco Seals played 225. Major League Baseball (MLB) teams today play just 162.

Though PCL teams drew huge crowds, California did not have the top level of pro sports until 1946. That was the year the Cleveland Rams football team moved to Los Angeles. The Rams had just won the National Football League (NFL) championship a month before moving.

The Rams' arrival in Los Angeles officially made California a major league state.

The Rams were a big hit in their new town. Soon they were regularly drawing crowds of more than 90,000 people. At the same time, Los Angeles was booming in population. Other championship-level teams took notice.

By 1957, the Brooklyn Dodgers baseball team had reached the World Series five times in eight years. The New York Giants had won the World Series in 1951 and 1954. But both had issues.

The Dodgers had a small stadium and wanted to expand. The Giants also struggled to draw fans to their ballpark. Both teams found a solution in California. In 1958, the Dodgers moved to Los Angeles, and the Giants moved to San Francisco. Though they were now 400 miles (644 km) apart instead of across town from each other, their **rivalry** remained one of the best in sports.

The floodgates had opened. Before long, there were five MLB teams in California. The Los Angeles Angels were founded as an **expansion** team in 1961. The Athletics moved to Oakland in 1968 from Kansas City, Missouri. And the San Diego Padres were added as an expansion team in 1969. All five teams still exist, though the Angels moved to nearby Anaheim in 1966.

Pro football in California has undergone many changes. The San Francisco 49ers, named after

▲ Like many California teams, the Golden State Warriors originally played in a different city.

the Gold Rush of 1849, were founded the same year the Rams moved to Los Angeles. But until 1950, they played in the All-American Football Conference. California got two new pro football teams in 1960. The Los Angeles Chargers and Oakland Raiders joined the new American Football League (AFL) that year. The Chargers moved to San Diego in 1961. Both teams thrived.

But in 1970, the AFL and NFL merged, and the Chargers and Raiders became NFL teams.

The Chargers remained in San Diego until 2017, when they moved back to the Los Angeles area. The Raiders made several moves. They moved to Los Angeles in 1982. Then they moved back to Oakland in 1995. And in 2017, they announced plans to move out of California and to Las Vegas, Nevada. The Rams have moved around, too. In 1995, they left for St. Louis, Missouri. The team played there for 21 years before moving back to Los Angeles in 2016.

Pro basketball is popular throughout California, as well. The state got its first National Basketball Association (NBA) team in 1960. That year, the Lakers moved to Los Angeles. The team previously played in Minneapolis, Minnesota, where it had won five league titles. In 1962, the Warriors became California's second team. They moved from Philadelphia to San Francisco. Today they are known as the Golden State Warriors.

In 1984, the San Diego Clippers moved north and joined the Lakers in Los Angeles. The next year, the Kansas City Kings moved to Sacramento.

CALIFORNIA'S BIGGEST WINNERS

Los Angeles Lakers 11 NBA titles

San Francisco 49ers 5 Super Bowl wins

Los Angeles Dodgers  5 World Series wins

Los Angeles Galaxy  5 MLS Cup wins

Los Angeles Sparks  3 WNBA titles

Los Angeles Kings 2 Stanley Cup wins

Accurate as of January 2018

The only NBA team to move out of California was the Houston Rockets, who left San Diego in 1971.

California doesn't get much snow or ice, but hockey has found a home there. The National Hockey League (NHL) expanded into the state with two teams in 1966. The Oakland Seals didn't survive, but the Los Angeles Kings did. Hockey grew further with the San Jose Sharks joining the league in 1991 and the Mighty Ducks of Anaheim (now the Anaheim Ducks) joining in 1993.

Two of the nation's newest leagues have a presence in California as well. Major League Soccer was founded in 1996. The Los Angeles Galaxy and San Jose Clash were two of the league's founding members. The Clash later became the Earthquakes, and in 2006 they moved to Houston, Texas. A new Earthquakes team was founded in 2008. The Galaxy briefly shared a

 Candace Parker and the Los Angeles Sparks won the 2016 WNBA title.

stadium with a team called Chivas USA, and in 2018 a new team, Los Angeles FC, began play a few miles away.

The Women's National Basketball Association (WNBA) was also founded in 1996. The league had original teams in Los Angeles and Sacramento. However, only the Los Angeles Sparks remain. The Sacramento Monarchs **folded** in 2009.

"MR. PADRE" TONY GWYNN

Few players have had as much of an impact on their home state as Tony Gwynn. Gwynn was born in Los Angeles on May 9, 1960, and grew up in nearby Long Beach. A two-sport star, Gwynn went to San Diego State University to play basketball. He soon switched back to baseball. The Padres drafted Gwynn, and he debuted for them in 1982. Gwynn then played his entire 20-year career in San Diego, earning the nickname Mr. Padre.

Gwynn was best known for his hitting. He had 3,141 career hits and won eight National League (NL) batting titles. His greatest season was in 1994. Gwynn was hitting .394 in August. Fans wanted to see if he could hit .400. No one had done that since 1941. However, a players' **strike** ended the season early.

Gwynn's 3,141 career hits for the Padres was nearly three times more than the team's next-best player.

Gwynn was also a great outfielder and won five Gold Glove Awards. In addition, he helped the Padres reach the World Series in 1984 and 1998.

After retiring in 2001, Gwynn returned to his **alma mater** as the baseball coach. In 2007, he was inducted into the National Baseball Hall of Fame. Gwynn died of cancer in 2014. He is still beloved in San Diego, where his No. 19 was retired and a statue was built in his honor.

CHAPTER 3

CALIFORNIA COLLEGES

When it comes to college athletics in California, two sports reign supreme: football and basketball. Several California schools have thrived in those sports.

College football in the state dates back to the 1880s. The University of Southern California (USC) played its first game in 1888. Since then, the Trojans have won 11 national titles and produced six **Heisman Trophy** winners.

The USC Trojans are often among the best teams in college football.

Across town, the University of California, Los Angeles (UCLA) has won just one national title. But the Bruins have a fierce rivalry with USC. The teams first played each other in 1929, and they have played every year since 1936.

Up north, it's all about the Big Game. That is the name for the rivalry between the University of California and Stanford University. The two teams play for the Stanford Axe trophy.

The most famous moment in the history of the Big Game was in 1982. Stanford took the lead with four seconds left in the game. That meant Cal would have to return the kickoff for a touchdown. During the return, the Stanford band marched onto the field, thinking the game had ended. But the play was still going. A Cal player had the ball and was sprinting toward the end zone. After running over a band member, he scored the game-winning touchdown. Known simply as "The Play," it was one of the most famous moments in college football history.

In basketball, UCLA rules the state. In fact, no school has won more national titles than UCLA.

USC VS. UCLA: TALE OF THE TAPE ◁

USC football and UCLA men's basketball are two of the most successful college programs ever. But how do they compare?

USC Football	UCLA Basketball
First season: **1888**	First season: **1919–20**
All-time winning percentage: **.704**	All-time winning percentage: **.692**
National championships: **11**	National championships: **11**
Conference championships: **38**	Conference championships: **37**
Pro Hall of Famers: **12**	Pro Hall of Famers: **5**

Accurate as of January 2018

From 1967 to 1973, the Bruins won eight national championships in a row. In addition, more than 80 Bruins have gone on to play in the NBA. However, USC's women's basketball team won national titles of their own in 1983 and 1984.

College baseball and softball are also popular in California. There are 24 **Division I** baseball programs in the state. There are also 20 Division I softball programs. No baseball program has won more national titles than USC. And no softball program has won more than UCLA. However, there are several successful programs from each sport in California.

Smaller sports thrive in California colleges, too. In fact, a 2017 study looked at how many US Olympians each college had produced. The top four colleges were all in California. Stanford led the list with 298 Olympians. Combined, Stanford

▲ Stanford swimmer Katie Ledecky (left) won four gold medals at the 2016 Olympics.

athletes had won 282 medals in a wide variety of

sports, including beach volleyball and water polo.

ALL-CALIFORNIA QB

Derek Carr's football career has taken him all over the United States. But his home base has always been California. Carr was born in Fresno and went to college at Fresno State.

While playing for the Bulldogs, Carr was one of the best quarterbacks in the country. As a senior in 2013, he won the Sammy Baugh Award as the best passer in the nation. He threw for more than 5,000 yards and had 50 touchdown passes. Only three other college quarterbacks had ever done that.

The amazing season led the Oakland Raiders to select Carr in the second round of the 2014 NFL Draft. He was given the chance to start right away in the NFL, playing all 16 games that season. The Raiders struggled, but Carr threw 21 touchdown passes and just 12 interceptions. He was even

⬩ Derek Carr celebrates after throwing a touchdown pass during a 2017 game.

better in 2015, throwing 32 touchdown passes. He also made his first Pro Bowl that year.

In 2016, Carr led Oakland to its first playoff appearance in more than a decade. He threw for nearly 4,000 yards and had 28 touchdown passes. He finished third in Most Valuable Player voting. In just three seasons, Carr had established himself as one of the best young quarterbacks in the NFL.

CHAPTER 4

A HUB FOR ALL SPORTS

California's sports history goes far beyond its most popular professional and college teams. The state's unique landscapes allow it to host a wide variety of sporting events. From winter sports in the mountains to surfing competitions on the coast, California has been home to countless competitions. In fact, the state is a global sports destination.

US track star Rafer Johnson lit the Olympic flame at the 1984 Summer Olympics in Los Angeles.

No sporting event is bigger than the Olympic Games. California has hosted the Games three times. The resort town of Squaw Valley, near Lake Tahoe, hosted the 1960 Winter Games. Those Games were famous for American hockey fans. Long before the 1980 "Miracle on Ice," the 1960 US men's hockey team upset the Soviet Union on its way to winning the gold medal in Squaw Valley. It is known as the "Forgotten Miracle."

Los Angeles hosted the 1932 and 1984 Summer Games. It is scheduled to host the Games again in 2028. Many famous Olympic moments happened in Los Angeles. In 1932,

➤ **THINK ABOUT IT**

What qualities do you think make a city a good fit to host the Olympic Games?

Babe Didrikson won three track-and-field medals there. She was one of the first women's sports stars. In 1984, Carl Lewis won four track-and-field medals in Los Angeles. He was the first American to do so since Jesse Owens in 1936.

The Los Angeles Memorial Coliseum was built for the 1932 Games. It was also used during the 1984 Games and is set to host events in 2028.

Between the Olympics, the Coliseum has hosted many other major events, including USC home football games. Both the Coliseum and the nearby Rose Bowl have hosted the Super Bowl. The Rose Bowl also hosts UCLA home football games and the annual Rose Bowl college football game. In addition, two World Cup soccer finals took place in the Rose Bowl. Both ended in dramatic shootouts. In 1994, Brazil beat Italy in the men's final. Five years later, the women's final featured the United States and China. A crowd of more than 90,000 fans saw the Americans win the World Cup there. It was the biggest crowd ever for a women's sporting event.

California also hosts many smaller sporting events. One sport with a particularly California feel is beach volleyball. While it has only been an Olympic sport since 1996, beach volleyball in

Brandi Chastain scores the winning goal for the US team at the 1999 Women's World Cup final in the Rose Bowl.

California dates back to the 1920s. Public courts started popping up in Santa Monica, and they now line the beaches. One of the sport's major tournaments takes place in Manhattan Beach every year.

Other parts of California host major golf and surfing tournaments. In the mountains, there is even enough snow to host skiing and snowboarding events.

CHAPTER 5

A STATE OF PLAY

With so much space and so many people, California is a state with a wide variety of cultures. People have come to California from all over the world. Their experiences have shaped the state in many ways.

Duke Kahanamoku introduced surfing to the state in 1912. Surfing had been popular in his native Hawaii since the 1400s. When locals saw Duke surfing, they wanted to try, too.

California is one of the world's top destinations for surfing.

Surfing became massively popular in the 1950s and 1960s. The Beach Boys sang about it, and surfing slang became popular around the world. Later, some California surfers came up with the idea of putting wheels on small versions of surfboards. Skateboarding was born.

Before skate parks, skaters used California's many hills and even empty swimming pools. In the 1980s, skaters started using video cameras to share their tricks and spread the sport's popularity. Skaters such as Tony Hawk fell in love with the sport this way. By the 1990s, skateboarding had its own international competitions such as the X Games.

Surfing also gave birth to snowboarding. The first snowboard was called the Snurfer—a combination of snow and surfer. Though snowboarding was invented in Michigan, it caught

🔺 California's Lake Tahoe is a popular spot for snowboarders and skiers.

on in California. Several famous ski resorts are in California's mountains.

While surfing and skating are popular all over the state, they are mostly associated with Southern California. That is where both sports developed. Northern California also has its own unique culture. Because the two parts of the state are so different, they have an ongoing rivalry.

This rivalry even extends to major pro sports. The Giants and Dodgers have a fierce rivalry, as do the Chargers and Raiders.

But there are rivalries within each region, too. The Giants and A's are located across the San Francisco Bay from each other. The teams are in different leagues, so they don't play often. When they do, it's a big deal. They met in the 1989 World Series, which was known as the Bay Bridge Series. It was named for the bridge that links San Francisco and Oakland.

California is a car-crazy state. Its big size and sprawling cities mean cars are the main way

> ## THINK ABOUT IT

Which sports are popular in your area? Why do you think they became popular?

Built in the 1930s, the Bay Bridge spans 8 miles (12 km) across the San Francisco Bay.

people get around. As a result, a lot of the state's rivals are linked by a roadway. When the Dodgers play the Angels, it is known as the Freeway Series. The teams' ballparks are linked by Interstate 5.

California was once part of Mexico, and the state still borders Mexico to the south. Millions of Mexican immigrants and their descendants live in California. This has great influence on the state.

Mexico's Aldo de Nigris celebrates after scoring a goal against Venezuela during a game in San Diego.

Mexican-American culture plays an important role in shaping California's culture, including the state's sports culture.

Soccer is more popular in Mexico than in the United States, and Mexican fans turn out for the sport in California. The Mexican men's national soccer team often plays matches in the state to sellout crowds. Even a 2015 **friendly** against

Ecuador drew 90,000 people to the Los Angeles Coliseum.

Mexican athletes in other sports are also very popular in California. In 1981, Mexican pitcher Fernando Valenzuela burst onto the baseball scene with the Dodgers. Not only did fans come out to Dodger Stadium to watch him, games were broadcast on TV in Mexico City. Valenzuela won the Cy Young Award as the NL's best pitcher, and the Dodgers won the World Series. More recently, Mexican soccer star Giovani dos Santos joined the Galaxy in 2015.

Many think of California as a laid-back state, with surfers and sunbathers everywhere. While surfing and beach culture are huge, California is home to so much more. Its sports fans are passionate and come from all over the world. There is a sport for everyone to watch or play.

FOCUS ON
CALIFORNIA

Write your answers on a separate piece of paper.

1. Write a sentence that summarizes California's culture, as discussed in Chapter 5.

2. Which team or event in California would you most like to watch? Why?

3. Which was the first NFL team in California?

    A. San Diego Chargers
    B. Los Angeles Rams
    C. San Francisco 49ers

4. Why don't the Giants and A's play each other very often?

    A. They are in different leagues.
    B. They play at different times of the year.
    C. The fans don't get along.

Answer key on page 48.

GLOSSARY

alma mater
A school that a person used to attend.

colonized
Settled in a new place and took control.

Division I
The top level of college sports in the United States.

expansion
When a sports league adds more teams.

folded
Closed a business.

friendly
A soccer match that doesn't count as part of a competition.

Heisman Trophy
The award given to the best college football player each season.

prospectors
People who search for valuable materials such as gold or oil.

rivalry
An ongoing competition between two players or teams.

strike
When people stop working as a way to demand better working conditions or better pay.

TO LEARN MORE

BOOKS

Dzidrums, Christine. *Clayton Kershaw: Pitching Ace.* Whittier, CA: Creative Media, 2014.

Watson, Stephanie. *Timeline History of the California Gold Rush.* Minneapolis: Abdo Publishing, 2015.

Whiting, Jim. *Los Angeles Lakers.* Mankato, MN: Creative Education, 2018.

NOTE TO EDUCATORS

Visit **www.focusreaders.com** to find lesson plans, activities, links, and other resources related to this title.

INDEX

Answer Key: 1. Answers will vary; **2.** Answers will vary; **3.** B; **4.** A